The Missing Link

The Missing Link

A SPIRITUAL GUIDE FOR
UNDERSTANDING ADDICTIVE BEHAVIORS

Susan V Kippen

The Missing Link
A spiritual guide for understanding addictive behaviors

Conscious Quest Press
PO Box 1074
Manomet, MA 02345
Email: susan@southshorenaturalhealing.com

Book cover design by
Leanne Lebow
brownleanne@hotmail.com

Cover and inside imagery © iStock by Getty Images

ISBN-13: 9780578187600 (sc)
ISBN-10: 0578187604
ISBN: 978-0-998-4963-0-6 (e)
Library of Congress Control Number: 2016921495
Manomet, MA

Disclaimer

THE INFORMATION CONTAINED WITHIN THIS book is for educational purposes and offers a mindful approach for honest participation with the self and the everyday processing of life experiences. Before beginning any new program or making use of any information from this book, it is recommended that you seek medical/psychological advice from your personal physician or licensed mental health provider. This book is not intended to be a substitute for any support program or medical advice or medical care that you are presently receiving or may need from a licensed mental health professional or a licensed physician. Readers should consult with their health care provider in any matters relating to health. The author does not assume and hereby disclaims any liability to any party for any loss, damage, or disruption caused by applied use of information contained in this book, errors or omissions, whether such errors or omissions result from accident, negligence, or any other cause. If you wish to make use of information contained in this book, you are taking full responsibility for your own choices.

Acknowledgments

I WOULD LIKE TO EXPRESS my gratitude to the individuals whose encouragement and support on a personal and professional level have led to the creation of this book.

Some special thanks go to my Aunt Ivy for her encouragement, support, and kindness.

I would like to thank Reverend Dick Fewkes for trusting in my capabilities and encouraging me along the way.

Also, much gratitude goes to my departed friend Dr. Henry Smith Rohrberg for his teachings, professional encouragement, and his dependable, enthusiastic invitation to share in the celebration of life.

For editing assistance, I am grateful to Joanne Desario and Pam Summa.

Also, my life and my work have been Divinely guided and for that, I am very grateful.

Introduction

THIS BOOK PROVIDES A MULTIFACETED in-depth view of the unconsciously driven behaviors within addictive patterns, along with a spiritual process for the potential of realizing wholeness within. Addictive behaviors come in many forms; a substance may or may not be involved. When looking at the habitual patterns within the unconscious mind, it is apparent that the programming is similar in most situations of dependence. The more entrenched the addictive role becomes, the more unconscious the choices and actions will be. Until individuals consciously recognize the limitations within their behaviors, they will continue to function in their habitual responses to life circumstances. Inward focus, mindfulness, is necessary for seeing and transforming the self. Without this, one will continue to cycle in unconsciously driven self-sabotage, self-doubt, disappointment, and struggle.

Many addiction programs are fragmented – incomplete on their own. For a likelihood of greater success, a multi-leveled approach is needed, one that combines a support plan to eliminate a substance, offers reprogramming through new learning, and mindful participation with a new experiential understanding. Additionally, an ongoing support system is needed and healthy complimentary choices.

This guide addresses the "Missing Link" that is needed to achieve wholeness with one's understanding and participation in "process." It breaks down the patterns that are at the foundation of addictive experience, in order to bring about a cohesive understanding of the limitations within the fragmented behaviors. Next, approaches to assist with change are presented, along with tools for greater self-awareness and "processing" capabilities. In order for individuals to change something within themselves, they must first experientially realize what is happening. Most often the addicted person functions from an unconscious foundation of fragmented processing capabilities due to inadequate learning, trauma, and/or suppressed abilities. In order to transform, one must learn how to see oneself and to learn the skills for effective processing. One's fragmented self needs to heal in order to transition beyond an addictive practice and into a conscious ability to negotiate the larger experience of life.

The information herein is intended to assist in the building of personal awareness, integrity, trust, confidence, and individuality. It is recommended that you read this entire guide. Otherwise, your understanding of the information will be fragmented and its use will be limited. Also, it is intended that this guide be read slowly with contemplation and reflection, so that it becomes experiential rather than simply intellectual. To access a deep understanding of the material, you must take your time with it.

—⟟—

May we all hold a torch of hope for one another, until each person can see it burning for themselves.

Contents

Section One

Understanding your behaviors

Understanding your behaviors

ADDICTIVE BEHAVIORS

ADDICTIVE BEHAVIORS CAN DEVELOP WITH or without the use of alcohol or chemical substances. They can present themselves in many forms: alcohol, use of electronics, video games, drugs, sex, gambling, shopping, drama, work, play, food, a chronic role (such as controlling others, pleasing others or being right), an activity, an emotional approach, etc. They can also develop as a means of escape from unresolved trauma. It is common for an individual to alternate between a variety of addictive behaviors, or if they let go of one, it may be replaced by another. The full capacity of human experience becomes diminished and controlled by the behavior through habitual, consistent use. The varied, spontaneous emotional expressions of the naturally occurring consciousness become secondary to the artificial state created by the habit. Once the dependency becomes an extreme routine part of one's practice, an individual's natural state will no longer be an experience of choice. It will feel unnatural and undesirable. The addictive behavior creates a false sense of control as it brings about a consistent state that dominates many expressions of self. This artificial buffer creates a veil between one's actions, the authentic self, and the experience of cause and effect. The action of automatic compulsive choice replaces conscious choice.

THE MISSING LINK

The missing link exists in one's inability to understand complete "process." We make rational sense of the world through our capacity to be present with and fully process our feelings, understandings, ideas, choices, and situations. Addictive behaviors are often a symptom of one's incapacity to adequately make sense of ongoing personal experiences within the context of life. They provide a symptomatic cycle that is used to escape the struggle of having limited tools for gaining clarity, understanding, and to consciously direct oneself from one choice to the next.

Many people who have addictive behaviors have not learned how to "process" in an in-depth way or to see themselves clearly. As a result, their individuality has not been adequately developed or becomes somewhat frozen. The full value of inward self-inquiry is not realized – it is often feared. The ability to clearly participate in one's experiences from start to finish with a sense of safety, curiosity, and enthusiasm is lacking. They have not fully learned the skills necessary to step into the unknown and discover, to honestly negotiate what works and doesn't work, and to trouble shoot in solo or in shared experiences. Instead, theory is often perceived as reality. This can lead to unhealthy patterns of perfectionism, competitiveness, egocentrism, co-dependency, belief in sameness, black and white thinking, and drama. Individuality is stagnated. For effective processing and personality building, one must experience the steps of curiosity, discovery, participation, negotiation, integration, and reflection repeatedly, over and over, as participatory experience continues. This process is an ongoing part of life.

The degree of one's capacity to fully participate in the actual unfolding of ongoing experience and discovery becomes more apparent when interpersonal situations are taking place. These types of situations require the ability to see oneself, to be present with others, to spontaneously choose, negotiate, and engage with ever-changing unknowns. When the ability to negotiate all the required steps of "process" is incomplete, a person will adapt into the limitations of one's learned skills and compensate for what has not yet been learned. This will be varied and unique within each person.

For example, one person may seek isolation or create busyness within the safety and comfort of set roles. When an individual's choices and actions are determined by a role, such as a professional position or a project, their inadequacies tend to be partially camouflaged or totally hidden. When the same skill set is used over and over in a particular context, the skill will become highly developed as it relates to the predictable routine. The lack of skills and understanding, within other levels of self, may not be obvious. The need to spontaneously negotiate and apply a wide range of interpersonal skills is decreased or even diverted through consistent participation in set roles. The roles become an addictive behavior. A relationship with rigid, imbedded rules will also provide the same effect as a role.

The role or rule makes the outcome of each choice and action appear more predictable. A free flowing interpersonal level of participation, does not easily blend with set roles. Instead, the levels of self, become compartmentalized. One's individuality within the varied levels of personality is not secure. A secure sense of self cannot stand on its own within the fluctuations and spontaneous experience of everyday life.

Another common scenario that might take place is when individuals have trouble committing to ongoing challenges. Their whole life or certain parts of their life may exist in a consistent state of transition. Relationships, jobs, and living situations may change constantly. They may appear to be confident on the outside; however, on the inside they are terrified. They don't know how to challenge their own judgements around personal limitations and the instability of their own individuality. When people make choices to abruptly interrupt a present situation, the fantasies that exist within their ideas for change give them a greater sense of temporary, false control over themselves and their life. An idea for something different will temporarily disguise the fear of not knowing what to do for themselves in the situation that already exists. The ideas and efforts to attain something new will only bring temporary relief to the suffering; therefore, an interchange will be sought out repeatedly, over and over again. It may extend to new places to live, excessive shopping, the need for new clothes, friends, etc. All of it becomes compulsive with addictive behaviors playing out.

Where the need for a process or resolution is concerned, an idea cannot and will not effectively stand on its own without the movement that comes through inward participation with self and outward discovery with the unknown circumstances of life. The lack of understanding around personal roles and beliefs will lead to a sense of feeling trapped and the need to look for solutions from outside of oneself, through the efforts of another. It is only through inward participation that a person can realize their fears, gain personal wisdom, and find real solutions. Without this, judgement of self and others, blame, and resistance will be the result, leading to self-sabotage and the perceived need for rescue.

Once individuals learn that they can get others to rescue them, they are likely to harm themselves over and over. The sabotage is unconscious. Their behavior often evolves into a sense of entitlement, which allows them to transfer their sense of inadequacy and fear of the unknown onto someone else through blame. From their perspective, others are responsible for rescuing them and making them comfortable. The thinking itself becomes addictive through a dependent attachment to the entitlement and blame. However, none of this will change anything for them. One person's efforts cannot create a foundation for another individual. Each person must seek to experience more than what they think they already know from within the self and the situations that arise in the outer world.

In another type of scenario, a person may function in dominating and abusive patterns. Abusive patterns are often used to block one's options for personal flexibility around needs and the necessity to negotiate the challenging effects from the expressions of others. If an abuser cuts off the individuality of another, then he/she is not required to directly participate with, rationally adjust to, and negotiate his/her own personality or behavior, or to directly experience his/her inability to process oneself in the unknown challenges of life. Very little learning can take place. A false sense of safety, predictability, and control will lead to a dependency with the unhealthy behaviors.

Another version may be with people who enter into a relationship where they allow someone else to have complete control over them financially, so that they don't have to participate for themselves, because they do not believe in themselves. The possibility of participation in the process of discovery may repeatedly trigger a fear of failure or doom. The resulting sense of inadequacy will often be transferred into a habitual practice that brings temporary relief and escape. As an example, this could translate into a feeling of being deprived – an excessive, urgent need for food. The unhealthy effect of overeating and the confusion from the compulsiveness will only lead to even less belief in self.

In all the above scenarios, one continues to exist in limited ways. Solutions are sought from outside of the self rather than going within. A sense of discontent, powerlessness, confusion, resistance, and struggle may be present. The circumstances and reactions to the situations enable the person to stay the same. An ongoing process for making rational sense of life and creating individuality on all the varied levels of self is just not known. Such individuals may be afraid or terrified of what they don't know within their own possibilities. With an incomplete understanding of the limitations of their own programming and of cause and effect, the same scenarios just keep cycling over and over. Addictive, compulsive behavior disguises one's pain and discomfort over not knowing how to participate within the self. There are endless ways that habitual behavior attempts to conceal a fragmented experience of self.

Where there is a lack of ability to process, there are often ineffective attempts to do so in one's own head with pieces of theory or untested ideas. If a theory is held as reality and applied only to one's thinking and projections, then it becomes active fantasy. When this is the case, there is no awareness of a bridge – of how to take steps to transition or test out the legitimacy of theory. There is no effective means of discovering how the theory may or may not be applied or integrated as purposeful knowledge and experience. Despite the lack of knowing, one's consciousness will still attempt to create completion through various means. Sometimes circular thoughts will go around and around in one's head. This brings a false sense of safety while at the same time creating inner turmoil, a struggle, and stress. When the internal stress escalates, it may be cast on to others through drama in another attempt to get rid of it. However, this will also prove to be ineffective, since real solutions exist through curious, flexible, and direct participation. (A more comprehensive description of drama is provided further along in the guide.) An unclear understanding of how to share and access information leads to guarded participation, which in turn does not allow one to negotiate or perceive the larger picture of a situation and of self. When the individuals have difficulty honestly and spontaneously participating, surrendering, receiving, and testing the unknown, while creating boundaries, they will have resistance which acts as a barrier and blocks their ability to spontaneously venture into the unknown. The wholeness and substance of an experience cannot be received. The steps for discovery are brought to a halt.

WHAT IS RESISTANCE AND WHAT CAN I DO ABOUT IT?

When addictive behaviors are present, there is a predominant tendency to attempt to keep set modes of familiar, comfortable experience in place. The challenges that come from the unpleasant, unexpected, or unfamiliar variations of self and life are avoided. Resistance is a consequence of this.

This struggle is developed from a judgement of something that one imagines will or will not come about in relation to the possibility of making a choice. Consequently, the ability to participate in a required experience is hindered. This further progresses into an anxiety from a desire to predict, rejection of not knowing, a discomfort from the anticipated emergence of spontaneous needs in self and others, and the necessity to honestly negotiate the experience. There is a procrastination or attempt to delay an alternate experience. This does happen to some degree for everyone; however, it can be much more prevalent for those with addictive behaviors.

Know that every new occurrence is different than everything else that has ever taken place before; so no one cannot predict or realize an actual situation until they are in it. Since the person has not yet participated in an event, the event is not the problem. The suffering comes from the ideas that individuals personally develop in connection to a possible choice. This puts a barrier in place that stops them from participating in the full essence of the choice and the discoveries that can come from an unplanned, difficult, or new experience. It may feel like the struggle is something separate from you; however, you created it. Let's look at an example of how this may play out. When this constrained approach is present in one's programming, it often carries over and defines one's capacity to fully process oneself in a wide range of areas. It can affect everything from decision making, to effective communication and negotiation, and the way that individuals identify with one another in relationships. Let's look at an example of what could occur.

In this situation, the person has a weight problem. She was just informed by her physician that she has high blood pressure and is at risk for a heart attack or stroke. This individual tends to overeat, eat when she is upset, and to eat unhealthy foods. Upon hearing this medical report, the patient subconsciously judges herself and imagines that the doctor is also judging her. Shame surfaces. Due to an inability to participate directly with her own initial feelings, she reacts further with fear and anger. She feels a need to escape from any possible consideration of the news. The patient wants to leave the doctor's office and avoids the necessity to directly engage with it. She is desiring a different kind of experience. A wall of resistance has been created. Because this becomes her primary inner experience, she is unable to process the information in the context of cause and effect and real possibilities. The information did not create the inner barrier; she created it with her thoughts and emotions. The woman leaves the physician's office, gets in her car, eats some chocolate, and temporarily feels better. The judgement, projection, fear, and resistance blocked access to a conscious pathway for self-inquiry, recognition of cause and effect, or choice from real possibilities. To resolve this conflict, one must bring the focus inward to witness the self with curiosity. Once a person immerses them self in the substance of an experience, clarity and wisdom will come.

WHAT DOES IT MEAN TO "PROCESS?"

To begin processing, one starts with a feeling, an idea or piece of experience, and some sense or recognition of where that sits in the context of reality. One is present within their own spontaneous internal experience. There is a willingness to experience one's immediate situation whether it is pleasant or unpleasant. If one is stuck in resistance, reaction, or projection, it is acknowledged with intentional inquiry. A decision is made to move through it by making more choices and taking action one step at a time. There is a sense of cause and effect and an awareness of one's responsibility of choice. There is a curiosity, an ability or need to see that there is more to any situation than what meets the eye. There is a recognition that not knowing or being wrong is a rational, acceptable part of the human experience. This creates ongoing opportunities for people to discover and learn. Some or perhaps many steps are needed to courageously inquire, investigate, and try on many pieces of reality to see what fits, how they fit best, or if they don't fit at all. One recognizes that the self does not exist in a set or fixed way. Through participation, new developments and discoveries take place, just as much internally as they do externally with the world. Abilities become known and developed, while limitations are realized. Rational understanding makes it possible to know where to participate and where not to participate. Boundaries are made as needed. Pathways for rational discovery – for relief of pain and suffering – are sought out through possibilities that can lead to real solutions. One's awareness of steps is recognized in the context of ideas, goals, and movement while mindfully proceeding one step at a time. A trust and confidence in self and in life develops through participation. The world is not a scary place with dead ends – it is a place of adventure, challenges, choices, and discovery.

Of course, the ability to "process" does not bring perfection. There is still fear, distrust, doubt, not knowing, pain, etc., but these things are not a constant in one's foundation or sense of self. They are not a consistent governing factor in one's decision making. Instead, there is the courage to walk through each step and allow the experience itself to show one the wisdom. If individuals are constantly attempting to control the unfolding, then they will block their own ability to receive the authentic knowledge that comes through full participation. Participation with life and people is needed on all levels.

WHAT IS NEEDED FOR HEALING AND TRANSFORMATION TO TAKE PLACE WITH ADDICTIVE BEHAVIOR?

First, an individual must make a decision for change. If a substance is being used, such as alcohol or drugs, this must be eliminated. It is not possible to access the full self when a substance is being consumed. Then, in any type of addictive situation, one must be completely honest about the reality that has been created, behaviors and beliefs that are present, the choices made, and the roles that have been activated with the addictive behavior. With honesty, this will be discovered as you take forward steps with your commitment to become more self-aware and whole. Any trauma must be processed with the assistance of a professional. Along with this, healthy support must be accessed. In this way, you learn how to trust, be safely seen by others, receive from a basis of truth, surrender to what "is" and to what is new and different, learn how to take responsibility for cause and effect, and discover and receive in an authentic way from others and from the outside world. This means full disclosure and open honesty. If secrecy is in place, one cannot fully participate with oneself or the situation, or have access to all available possibilities. Honest participation with self and others leads to greater personal knowing, the capacity to ask for forgiveness and to forgive oneself, compassion and self-love. No matter what the habitual practice is, similar behaviors are present in all of them to a greater or lesser degree.

For change to take place in any situation, addictive or otherwise, one must know how to participate within the substance of one's own experiences to access an understanding. Then an awareness of truth can serve as a foundation within any choices for change. In this guide, the tendencies at the foundation of addictive behavior will be broken down to support an in-depth view for the individual. That will be the starting point for transformation. From there, supportive approaches for recognizing and participating in truth will be introduced. Inner inquiry and participation with new choices are up to you. It is recommended that you read this entire guide; otherwise, your understanding of the information will be fragmented and its use will be limited.

WHAT IS THE CONNECTION BETWEEN HONESTY AND DIVINE CONSCIOUSNESS?

Honesty expresses the truth of what "is" in the moment. Some truths are constant and some truths transition; however, they are the substance of your spiritual consciousness – the Omnipresence of All. This is a level of self where one can access clarity, compassion, and self-love. Intentional inner participation opens a pathway to Divine experience, wisdom, and inner guidance. The pure essence of creation always does exist within you. You are a spiritual being.

When you need help, be honest with yourself, and then bring your focus inward and ask for what you need from within the Divine of All. When you put your focus on an intention or idea with curiosity, you are establishing a relationship with it. Energy, creative consciousness, Divine Essence, and movement will naturally connect with your intention and give it life. It is within you as well as within everything else. Don't be afraid to acknowledge what you need at any given time and then ask. If you need clarity, an understanding of something, to take action, an experience of joy, etc., ask for it. Be as specific as possible and then let go. It is helpful to reach out through your own belief system. You may identify with Divine Essence, Buddha, God, Great Spirit, Jesus, Mary, Yahweh, Jehovah, Holy Spirit, Higher Self, All Knowing Consciousness, and so on. There are many religions and belief systems in the world. All of these belief systems, and others that have not been named, are pathways to Infinite Spirit, which transcends human experience. A daily spiritual practice will support the development of both self-awareness and spiritual-awareness. They are one in the same. I highly recommend a meditation practice. Some other practice options may include prayer, yoga, Chi Gong, Tai Chi, etc. A consistent spiritual practice supports a person's ability to be mindfully present in life and to be connected to "Source". This brings inner strength and is a means to keep oneself energetically clean.

HOW DO I RECOGNIZE A HEALTHY SUPPORT CONNECTION FROM OUTSIDE SOURCES?

Know that your primary source of safety for sharing with others comes through your own honesty. So, to effectively gain assistance, the honesty must be there. In this way, you are presenting yourself as a real person instead of a pretend projection of someone you think you should be. Others can only see and support you when you are your own authentic self. This can be uncomfortable at times, but that is a way of life that will transition you into a place of more learning and deeper knowing. It is an important piece of intimacy with yourself, life, and others. Outside support from skilled individuals and intimate connections are important.

When seeking a professional, such as a traditional or holistic therapist, look for recommendations from others, and then schedule an appointment to see if you feel a connection with the individual. Is there a good rapport that goes back and forth? Twelve step meetings can also be invaluable. When you commune with like-minded people, the energy within your intentions will become magnified. If you don't have transportation, Twelve Step programs can also be accessed on the Internet at www.intherooms.com. Groups that share in a mutual interest can be beneficial on many levels, as they create a source of community. If you have a specific religious belief, then a church environment can be another source of community. Try out numerous sources, and then decide upon the ones that you like the best.

From within your personal life, see if you can identify someone you trust as a support person. Your best option is someone who has compassion, is willing to see where you are in your experience, and will encourage and validate you when you take steps. If you go off track, perhaps this person could remind you of the relationship between action and consequence, your intentions, and possibilities and choices for a next step. Remember, you are learning to perceive and approach life in a different way. Your advocate should have a good foundation in "process" and an ability to see the larger picture.

Do not choose someone who is critical, judgmental, dramatic, or consistently negative, or one who would want to take over and dominate your experience for you. Your support person needs to understand that change takes place through you as you take many steps. Change does not instantly come about through an idea alone. A support person who believes that it does will be unconsciously supporting good/bad, black and white thinking. If someone is anchored in that type of programming, the feedback that is offered will be discouraging rather than encouraging. It will reinforce a sense of incapability and failure. Hopefully, your adviser can share in your vision, be understanding, celebrate steps with you, be curious to find solutions with you when you ask for help, be firm, but not critical, and redirect you if you become lost.

WHAT IS COMPULSIVE BEHAVIOR?

This is a primary behavior pattern that plays out in situations of addictive behavior. A compulsive choice occurs when decisions come from a basis of desire, rather than from a conscious awareness of the logical, rational option of choice and consequences. Most often, one does not have the ability to perceive a possible outcome when a compulsion is actively playing out.

The compulsion itself is like an encapsulated, limited piece of consciousness; it is not connected to one's larger reality and life. It is birthed out of a combination of distorted perceptions which may include: fear, shame, guilt, judgement, as well as an inability to fully process one's experiences, possibilities, and place in life. There is often a sense of feeling trapped by shame and guilt, because a healthy means of processing through it is unknown. This culminates in an urgent desire for immediate gratification and escape from discomfort – hence, the compulsion. The experience becomes contained within itself and takes on a life of its own. When it arises, the individual most often does not see it with the rational mind until the behavior is well under way.

Even then, it is often not seen. There are no other options of choice that immediately sit alongside the compulsion. A desire to escape dominates. Once the action is in motion, a desire for emotional and/or chemical fulfillment intensifies as the experience of the "Will" is activated in a harmful way. At this point, the person may glimpse the possibility of consequences, but they seem far away, and therefore they do not feel real. The consequences of the compulsive act are not connected to a recognizable "process" in one's programming. When harmful results do come about, the person who created the outcome often becomes confused, fearful, shameful, angry, and feels powerless. There is usually a desire to further escape or simply disassociate. One doesn't know how to fully assimilate what has happened in a rational, connected manner, so at this point the individual feels like a bad person. The mind imagines that it must be someone else's fault, so there is a tendency to blame others. The more a compulsion is carried out, the more one subconsciously identifies with it, until the person becomes a limited, encapsulated piece of consciousness.

The active experience may be like the analogy of individuals who would be contained in a small room during their upbringing. Their ability to perceive and choose would be limited to their experience in that room. If they were suddenly sent out into the world, their understanding and relationship to everything outside of that room would be foreign. There would be no point of reference or ability to negotiate cause and effect or to understand how to negotiate their own potential in relation to the outside world. This would have to be learned, a step at a time, through curiosity and participation with the unknown. A compulsion is created in a similar fashion – through exposure to limited possibilities which are cut short by one's circumstances, fears, psychological defenses, desires, or chemical needs. A compulsion is created through participating repeatedly with an action that one associates with (false) safety and some sort of fulfillment. It consists of fear, an impulse to escape, and gratification through the action. This is very black and white. It is not connected to logic. The either/or essence of this behavior can be pervasive throughout one's manner of processing or relating to life.

Because a compulsion is not connected to logic, there is no recognition of a process associated with it. The accompanying emotional reactions at its foundation are perceived as a threat. This is where the desire to escape comes in, and then a successful temporary departure brings fulfillment and a false sense of safety. The compulsion is a vehicle for escape – the getaway car. The fear of not knowing and the inability to perceive possibilities and process shame and guilt created it. It has no conscious, logical, or practical anchor in the context of one's life. The useful, purposeful place for fear and shame goes unseen. They are not gracefully integrated in one's experience. When these feelings occur, they are fragmented and their value is not recognized.

Within healthy processing there are multi-layered associations with cause and effect, which give a person space to see what they are doing. Because of the multi-layered associations, it is easier to see one's possible choices alongside consequences and other possibilities. On the other hand, no logical associations of cause and effect or complete problem-solving abilities connect to a compulsion; it is not anchored. It is like a presence within itself. It can arise quickly, go unseen at first, then begin acting to carry out a desire before the conscious mind has an opportunity to catch it. It does not have any experience of participatory space connected to it within the psyche. There are no steps developed with it. Thus, a repeating cycle gets set up with this experience, and one's fear and fear of shame feed upon themselves over and over. If one were to develop the ability to witness oneself through repeated inner watching, he/she would discover these layers and more.

The solution for transforming compulsive behavior must come from the inside. One must embrace a deeper understanding of his/her history and develop a mindful relationship with self (one's inner experience or authentic identity) and the possibilities for greater discovery in life. One must challenge fears in relation to "not knowing," and then wherever there is resistance, challenge it through honest participation. Through an understanding of one's behaviors, feelings, authentic needs, goals, along with a practice for taking steps of discovery, an integration of the fragmented parts of self becomes more likely, along with the development of new life skills and individuality. Also, as the compulsions are challenged through witnessing and the introducing of rational possibilities, they become more anchored. The inner watching must take place over and over again. The more the compulsions are witnessed, the more your beliefs and reactions will rise up to be seen. Continued participation in this practice will allow the compulsion to expand – to open up and connect with other parts of one's psyche. Eventually, compulsions can be reduced to simple desires with rational choices available alongside of them. By means of honest participation, greater skills for self-awareness are built, and a bridge gets created with the outside world.

WHAT IS BLACK AND WHITE THINKING?

Black and white thinking is a form of compartmentalized thinking. Ideas or concepts do not have variables attached to them or a pathway for discovery. They are boxed up. They come from theory and fragmented experience. The ego has a strong relationship with this type of perception. With black and white thinking, the ability to bridge individual choice and outcome with the larger picture of reality and participation in continued possibilities has not been learned. Responsibility for "not knowing" has never been made safe, and curiosity toward the unknown in situations of spontaneous need is not free flowing. There is a "disconnect" with spontaneous curiosity, discovery, and creativity within each occurrence of choice and outcome. This programming leads to a very compartmentalized approach to life.

This can interfere with one's ability to stay present in the ongoing process of taking the steps necessary to fulfill goals. There is a disconnect with the value of each step and lack of confidence to spontaneously problem solve or negotiate for oneself. Efforts are not made to creatively fulfill an outcome. Possible steps are often approached with resistance or impatience. Alternate possibilities are seen as an intrusion or threat, while the idea of the outcome brings a separate sense of excitement. If a sense of value is not equally inherent in the idea, exploratory steps, and the goal, then there will be a lot of resistance and struggle with little drive to keep going. This leads to a boxed-up perception of success or failure along with a fear of one's goals. Theory or the idea of something becomes more comfortable than the unknowns of new experience.

It is common in either/or behavior to see fixed labels used for describing an experience rather than descriptive words that are more fluid. You can see the compartmentalized fixed nature of words like good, bad, weak, strong, mother, father, hot, cold, etc. Specific associations are inherent in the suggested meaning due to the historical use. On the other hand, there is evidence of a "process" in words such as inquisitive, challenging, domineering, understanding, supportive, limited, extraordinary, interesting, etc. These words can open one's curiosity and encourage a first hand, individual experience.

Transition out of limited perceptions involves conscious, curious participation with a multitude of ongoing choices and possibilities, as they relate to one's inner world and the outer world. Think of the choices as steps of discovery. A state of curiosity will invite new possibilities, encourage one to explore through choice and build personal trust of self. This will lead to a greater ability to love oneself, as well as the ability to love others. Participation with steps from the unknown provides ongoing healthy challenges, breakthrough, and understanding. Self-nurturing comes about in this process as one receives the newness of life.

WHAT IS UNHEALTHY EGO?

This is the part of the self that thinks it knows everything; it wants to be able to predict, and it attempts to force one's familiar approach, perceptions, and ideas into one's own experiences and onto others. It is attached to theory – black and white thinking. It tries to contain, possess, and be in charge. It also arises in the form of reactions and defenses in an effort to block personal discovery and changes within the self. If one's "witnessing self" is not present, the ego can sabotage a person's access to wisdom, growth, and change.

WHAT IS SECRECY AND DENIAL?

This takes place when one consciously or unconsciously decides to hide experiences, choices, perceptions, and be-haviors from self and others. The choice to look inward with honesty supports safety and the ability to see and understand the self in the context of life. If something is kept separate from the outer world or distant from self, then it does not feel as real as if someone had witnessed it and mirrored it back to the person through acknowledgment. When something is witnessed by another person, it becomes more anchored as a reality. This creates more accountability and ownership with conscious, ongoing choices. Without inward inquiry and reflection, a personal understanding of self will be limited – many aspects of a person's behavior will go unseen. Recognition of truth brings about a deeper understanding of and relationship with each individual choice and outcome.

Sometimes the act of secrecy is not consciously chosen at all. It is not recognizable to the one experiencing it. This is often referred to as denial. When it happens subconsciously, the person is governed by fears and lack of experience with the self and individual process. One's moral consciousness will often encourage inward participation, while a fear of the self or the unknown may compulsively bring it to a halt. People who are in denial are not capable of perceiving what may appear to be obvious to others.

When conscious choice activates secrecy, the person does have some capability to rationally process the truth of a reality, but still has fear, shame, and guilt that govern their choices. Since they do not understand their own reactions and defenses, the need to hide takes over. Their perceptions are disjointed and therefore distorted. They may dismiss or pretend that something is not real or did not take place, but deep down they know that it did. They do not have a full understanding of what is happening. Both scenarios create a divide or disconnect between the experience and the wise authentic self.

WHAT IS IT TO PERSONALIZE?

The act of personalizing takes place when you merge your own experience of self with misinterpreted pieces of interpersonal exchange that are being witnessed or shared with another individual. There is often a perception of inferiority or superiority toward the other person, which generally leads to a struggle when the personalities appear to merge through inaccurate interpretation and a transferred sense of responsibility. The natural boundaries of individuality cannot be seen. Consequently, the one who is personalizing takes on the role of discrimination, perhaps condemnation, and a false responsibility for assessing or changing the person they are struggling with. The one who is personalizing believes that the unique expressions of someone else can compromise or victimize their experience in some way. An expectation for unrealistic accountability, understanding, and support may be transferred onto the other person. The one who is projecting has unknowingly handed over their personal option of choice and trust to the other individual.

The responsibility for active choice, required for self-awareness, self-care, discovery, and growth has been unconsciously given up. A dependency has been created. In the moment, one only sees the projected ideas of choice that have been transferred onto the other person. One has given up the power of their own freewill for individual choice.

Another version of this pattern can be recognized when one worries and imagines someone else to be personalizing something about oneself. They may project the notion that another individual may judge an idea, choice, or action that was presented or shared. Once the fear of judgement is activated, through the worry, it will lead to an internal reactive sequence of fear toward the idea of judgement, and worry about possible blame and anger from the other person. An individual may become consumed with repetitious fantasies of defensive internal arguments playing out over and over. The mind attempts to step ahead to prepare a defense against the unknown. Again, a sense of safety that comes from the ability to make honest spontaneous choices within the natural unfolding of authentic experience is unknown.

Simply said, if one believes that another person's perceptions, judgements, words, or actions can alter, replace, or change who they are on the inside, then they are personalizing. They are dependent upon another person to be a certain way, so that they can be a certain way. Once a person believes this, they then feel that the other person is responsible for their well-being. This perception can only exist through fantasy – who you are is who you are, unless you choose to alter or change yourself.

Let's look at an example of what could occur when two people are personalizing. For equality and healthy sharing, a situation that involves some joint decision making and clear communication is needed. We'll take the instance of two people who are in the beginning stages of a relationship. Perhaps they each have addictive and/or resistant patterns that limit their ability to process in real time.

In the initial stages of their experience, they feel mostly happy; there is a sense that they are perfect for one another. The couple has not yet experienced the real-life challenges that come from negotiating the uniqueness of individual personalities. This may or may not be recognizable to them. Their perceptions of individuality, at this point, are based in theory more than reality. To date, the couple has been arranging their time together in fun and exciting ways. There has been little negotiation with their shared unique inner experiences, which come with a sharing of everyday life. Now, the start of a required transition period comes along. The natural variations of life begin to seep in and influence reactive behavioral tendencies.

The couple has chosen to get together. Perhaps, on the same day, the man feels overwhelmed with the need to complete some work obligations and ready his home for guests who are coming to stay for a week. The woman is anticipating that the couples' planned experience will be as it had previously been – mutually adventurous and pleasant. Until this time, each person seemed to be in a similar mental/emotional place. They appeared to be mirrors of one another – the *same*. Now, due to a commitment to fulfill personal obligations, the man is more inwardly focused, constricted, and less inclined to be spontaneously free. As the contrasting intentions play out, the woman is conflicted over how to implement her predetermined expectations – how to replicate what had previously taken place. She becomes irritable, acts disappointed, and has a tone of blame in her remarks.

The man becomes confused. He is unclear about how to negotiate his needs and the new mix of feelings that are occurring, so he reacts with defensiveness. He continues in his attempts to fulfill the responsibilities at hand. At this point, they both personalize their partners' unanticipated reactions, feel rejected, create blame, and internalize a drama around the situation. The woman separates herself into the other room; her interactions become more reserved. She has let her expectations and perception of the other person alter her own ability to participate freely with confidence. Now, the man feels confused and more defensive. His reactions mostly remain inside of himself and he feels trapped. All of this leads to a struggle between them. Neither one of them participates with direct, open-ended questions, but instead, they end up making statements that are interwoven with blame. They end up resistant toward one another – stuck in their own perceptions of being victimized.

He and she both perceive that they have been compromised by the other person's behavior. They have each given up the possibility of participating with their individuality. Each one of them has taken on false responsibility for what they accurately and inaccurately perceive in the others' behavior. Their sense of well-being became dependent upon what the other person was doing. Each one of them personalized the others' behavior. They lost their objectivity, their ability to be curious, and to see the basic facts within themselves and the real adjustments needed to make the situation work. Neither one recognized the actual conflict.

To resolve this, they need to negotiate some variations of personal individuality and the unique needs that were created in the immediate conditions, along with available choices. The circumstances were not conducive for the same inner experiences to take place. Both parties started out with different intentions and distinct inner experiences. Neither one was wrong; they just didn't consciously recognize what was happening. There was an individual need for each person to bring their focus inward to access clarity in regard to personal reactions. Then an open discussion and adjustments needed to take place regarding their intentions, feelings, needs, and real possibilities per the actual circumstances, instead of desires. In this way, conscious choices could be made instead of unconscious reaction.

WHAT IS DRAMA?

Drama takes place when pieces of reality are taken out of context and are intertwined with the personal agenda of one or more people, resulting in distortion of truth and the attempt to have dominance over another person or situation. The perception and experience of individual boundaries becomes lost. Drama creates a distraction that prevents people from discovering the larger truth from within themselves and any situation. It does not invite an awareness of individual diversity or the unique experience within each person. An illusion or belief in sameness, separation, isolation, and inequality is suggested, encouraged, and projected with one's words and actions. Drama is *devoid* of purposeful participation in truth. It reinforces self-righteousness and a belief in victim and assailant roles. It creates confusion around individual identity and always spirals into the illusion of power through judgement and blame. Often, it is carried out behind someone's back, outside of the experience that provided the trigger, in the form of gossip or sadistic, passive bullying. With this approach, it is not possible for understanding, equality, sharing, discovery, or learning to take place. The fear of not being right and an aversion to anticipated shame is always present. A healthy understanding and experience of shame is unknown. Fear and fragmented perceptions fuel a cyclical need for allies who will validate one's skewed perceptions. This behavioral programming does not support healthy change, negotiation, or understanding. It does not support one's ability to perceive real possibilities for resolution of a problem. Repetitive participation in shared judgement leads to false fulfillment, and false fulfillment leads to addiction to the fragmented process. Consequently, choices for sharing and participation are based in fear, judgement, and blame instead of intentions for real solutions and purposeful experience. The defenses against shame block one's accessibility to purposeful choice.

This approach is not sustainable, because the wholeness of truth is not present. If the entire methodology is threatened, this will often lead to reactive anger as attempts are made for a renewed grasp of the illusionary experience. The following is an example how addiction to drama might get developed and play out.

This example involves a woman called Libby, who was unsupported around individual development when growing up. The primary focus was on survival. Most of the families in her community were better off financially and seemed happier. At an early age, she developed envy toward those who knew how to take care of themselves or who exhibited extravagance. Without guidance and support, she did not learn the steps for processing her emotions, needs, and choices in the context of ongoing life. As a result, her imagination led her to believe that someone else should be able to create what was needed for her. Because others were not participating for her, she felt like something was being done to her.

She had a relative Sarah, who, unlike Libby, recognized the need to participate for herself in life. This relative had vision, took purposeful action, sought to be mindful, and embraced life as an unlimited experience of discovery, manifestation, and learning. It was very natural for Sarah to bring kindness and acceptance to others while influencing unity. She functioned from the heart and strived to see value in everyone. Libby wanted to be like her.

She wanted to have what Sarah had; however, she did not recognize a process that would enable her to create for herself. She did not recognize the essence of equality with individuality. This led to more envy as she unsuccessfully attempted to mimic Sarah. She did not know that the solution was to focus inwardly, to directly understand her own needs, to address her fears, discover options, and take many steps into the unknown to learn and create first hand.

Eventually Libby felt ineffective, thereby developing greater rivalry and bitterness toward Sarah. Instead of bringing her focus inward to see the truth, her resentment toward Sarah escalated through drama. Sarah confronted the unkind behavior; however, it was met with hostility and went unheard. Libby made unsavory attempts to turn others against Sarah. Libby's resentments led to a conquest to discredit Sarah's very being – her wholeness as a person.

The ongoing struggle brought heartache and suffering to Sarah. She became hyper focused on the truth while believing that, "if others could only participate in it, then the divisions would end." She had personalized the conflict. Many mornings, upon waking, Sarah would struggle – feeling powerless – she would pray or reflect, looking for insight – a way to create harmony. She talked to other relatives and requested that they take a stand in the truth on her behalf. However, no one did. They were afraid to take a stand with someone who had a habit of persecuting others – afraid of being bullied, judged, dominated, or discarded. They kept pretending and enabling. Fear took away their voices. Relatives understood the wrong. However, they did not perceive their own personal roles with the conflict. There was no ability to completely process it. The gossip, distortions, and lies continued.

Eventually, Libby married into money. She lived in a big house and had a lavish lifestyle; however, she was still not happy. She developed a shopping addiction to relieve her torment. It only gave momentary escape. Sarah continued to be a constant reminder of what Libby was missing inside of herself. Just the thought of her brought discomfort. Libby developed obsessive thoughts about Sarah that were filled with the desire to dominate her with self-created judgmental fantasy.

Libby had regular holiday gatherings at her home. Sarah was not invited. Her presence would have represented a conflict between pretense and truth. It would have been impossible for Libby to comfortably maintain her self-created story, which conflicted with the authenticity of reality. The truth was the enemy and pretend was her friend. She was lost in a cyclical dramatization that held herself and all other participants hostage. She could not acknowledge a wrong; she was afraid to expose the shame and the void within herself. At all cost, Libby succumbed to her fears; subconsciously, she needed to hide the emptiness and the anxiety of not knowing herself from others. She continued to compulsively share distortions to accommodate her need for denial. She could not see herself.

From other relatives, Sarah continued to hear of Libby's malicious accusations toward her. Whenever possible she respectfully addressed Libby about these stories, but was met with hostility and defensiveness. For Libby, the discomfort of the confrontation only fueled more conflict and desire for drama as she attempted to discard it through allies. Sarah finally understood that no resolution was possible with Libby or the relatives. The tremendous suffering that she felt eventually brought her focus inward. She realized that the truth could stand on its own within herself, within her own identity. Her wholeness was not dependent upon anyone else participating there. The words or intentions that came from someone else could not make decisions for her identity or alter her. The Divine "within" brought the wisdom and awareness that she needed. With this knowing, she just witnessed from afar and maintained her experience of individuality. Sarah had surrendered. Peace and harmony had come.

Libby continued to function in a fragmented fantasy that kept her from mindfully participating with the larger reality of life. She identified with the practice of getting attached to fragments of information that fit her desires and reinforced her fears. Her perceptions became distorted through her imagination. She did not know that she had the option to share directly in truth and discover beyond her reactive attachments. The fear of not knowing, of being wrong, led to a constant void within. She backed away from the possibility of learning from challenges and resolving conflicts. She had developed resistance. Solutions were not created and an understanding was not reached. There was no ability to stay with a process. Instead, she got momentary fulfillment from the emotional charge of inner reactions. Because she functioned from fragmented processing capabilities, Libby was engaged in a constant struggle with either/or, black and white perceptions fueled by cyclical judgement, fear, and blame. This limited behavior led to powerlessness and the act of giving up the option to experience a more comprehensive awareness with reality and her authentic personal identity. This false sense of resolution was not sustainable, so it had to be repeated to no end. It was an addictive behavior. Her persistent fragmented processing could not bring about understanding, fulfillment, resolution, completion, or the wisdom that comes by virtue of honest participation with self and others.

May you live in the truth - it is your greatness.

WHAT IS BELIEF IN SAMENESS?

The belief in sameness comes from projected rigid ideas about how experiences or people should be, based on what one has already experienced or is presently witnessing. This occurs when someone takes what they see within themselves or someone else and imagines and expects that it should be the reality in both places. Such fixed projections lack spontaneous curiosity and creativity. This comes from a lack of trust in the unknown, a lack of living in the experience of the natural unfolding, which invites the process of discovery and integration into the diversity of life. When one's perceptions stop at an idea or theory, either a sense of inferiority emerges, or the ego jumps in, in with a role of superiority. This reinforces the illusions of predictability and unrealistic rules. Because sameness creates fixed ideas, one's sense of safety gets wrapped up in them. As a result, individuals project these fixed ideas out onto other people in an attempt to create comfort for themselves. Without this imagined comfort, there is an imaginary sense of personal assault that comes from within when differences are perceived. This can lead to fear, judgement, anger, impatience, competitiveness, and inner struggle.

Expectations of sameness are not always inappropriate. In the case of particular groups of people who wish to be treated with equal respect, sameness is fitting on a basic human level. This argument comes up in the workplace around equal pay for the same job performance among the sexes and races. In this type of healthy example, it is simply equality. Sameness has a place when considering equal rights for people of different genders, races, religions, and so on. However, it does not have a place when expectations are created to distract one's awareness from the reality of natural diversity within the experience of each human being.

The opposite of "sameness" is diversity. Diversity is the natural law of life and creation. No two of anything are exactly alike, not people, trees, the weather, days, celebrations, and so on. When one realizes the ever-changing essence of everything, then the untruths within the perception of sameness dissolve, and the experience of unity in diversity is realized. Acceptance and appreciation of diversity naturally provide an experience of grace from within the essence of the Divine.

HOW CAN I TRANSITION OUT OF PERCEPTIONS OF SAMENESS?

The way to resolve this is to first create the intention to be aware of when you are imagining that someone else expects you to be like them, or when you are expecting another person to perceive, approach, or understand a situation exactly as you do. Then open your curiosity to see the person or situation exactly as it is – without bringing your own desires into it. Next, bring your focus inward to the self and take responsibility for whatever you were expecting of the person or situation. Accept that your understanding and perception of anything belongs only to you. If another person was expecting you to take on their experience, let them be responsible for it. Do not create a struggle in response to a passive or direct suggestion. If you create a defensive, judgemental, or competitive role in response to the personal experience of another, then you will be overstepping boundaries and taking on inappropriate responsibility for them. Be aware of any inner desire to judge or struggle over what you see. Use your ability to question and witness the content of your thoughts, feelings, and beliefs. Now you can direct your mind inward or outward to view things as they actually are – without adding or taking away from what is there. In addition, use your curiosity to view the dissimilarities and consciously acknowledge that they are not a threat. When you recognize that you are the one making it difficult for yourself by blocking your ability to receive the unknowns and the whole truth of your experience, then you can choose differently. At this point, the option of choice can be recognized. You will have room for differences to co-exist in shared or witnessed experiences. With respect for equality with diversity, there is no room for competition, judgement, or struggle.

WHAT ARE BOUNDARIES?

Healthy boundaries are experienced through clear awareness of appropriate responsibilities between self and others. Boundaries acknowledge where individual experience,
space, process, choice, ideas, goals, likes, and dislikes begin
and end for each person. Boundaries create space between
each person's individual roles, choices, creations, and experiences. Making decisions for someone or creating judgements toward another person is an invasion of boundaries.
Examples of this become apparent in situations of drama
and impatience. If we have no responsibility with a situation
or a person's perceptions or choices, then there is no need to
create a goal oriented role. When we just witness, see things
for what they are without having the need to do anything
with what we see, this is a respect of boundaries. The individuality of another person is a pure offering of diversity
with which you can choose to participate or not. Equality
and boundaries go hand in hand. Respectful participation
and negotiation with the individual and the consciously
shared essence of equality and boundaries is a form of intimacy with self and others.

WHAT IS EQUALITY?

People often think of equality as sameness – the belief that
every person or situation should be experienced, seen, or

approached in the same way. But this kind of blanket approach is not the defining factor of equality. The essence of it is something much greater. In the wholeness of individuality, the parts of identity that are different from those in other people exist with equal respect right alongside whatever is similar. Equality as it relates to individuality is more about unity in diversity. It is more about acceptance through respect of the differences. When one recognizes true equality, the differences are just there, while at the same time, a person can choose whether to share or to contribute or not. Where one is capable and where there is opportunity to participate, one may choose to do so or not. There is no set expectation around obligation. There is no struggle created over what could have been, should be, might be, etc. When there is respect for the whole, then the similarities and differences are equal.

WHAT IS COMPETITION?

This takes place when one person feels threatened or diminished by the personal experiences or identity of another. In this situation, people often hold a subconscious belief that another person's life experiences, skills, perceptions, choices, and opportunities to participate can discredit them, diminish them, or take away their value. Another person's active presence becomes a threat. A person may feel unsafe due to the other individual being present and seen

– as though something is being done to them. Judgement is automatically created and projected inward to the self and outward to the other individual. Consequently, an immediate inner struggle gets created. This triggers an underlying sense of urgency, which often exists within the act of rivalry. The one who is threatened may urgently seek to retrieve from within their memory a similar or decidedly superior experience. It is then presented in opposition to what the other person has shared. This may involve talking over the individual who is sharing. There is a dependency and need for validation of one's identity from the outer world. Independence, personal power, and confidence are lacking in one's sense of individuality. The act of competition may be solitary or shared in a common situation.

When one feels competed against, one may attempt to resolve this self-induced feeling of disempowerment by internally formulating or attaching to a perception, idea, or experience that would make them feel equal or superior to the one being witnessed. If both parties get involved, the challenging behavior will be presented back and forth.

How can I effectively respond to competitiveness in myself and others?

First, if you feel competitive, direct your focus inward to discover the pieces of this imposing behavior. Notice if you might want to replace the other person's experience with your experience. You may feel that you want to be better than the other person. Perhaps you want to have the attention from others on you instead of on them. If this is the case, keep your focus inward and validate yourself as an individual; acknowledge that two people can be different and still exist equally. Now, refrain from pursuing the original challenge. If you have interrupted the other person, you might say something like, "I'm sorry. Please continue!" At this point, just listen, be present in order to notice that person as an individual. Realize that others have their own history which gives them their own way of perceiving and doing things. Note that at times the situation will be reversed.

If another person is challenging you with their attempts to override your experience, temporarily put all your focus on them. Let them know that you would like to finish speaking or sharing your story and they are welcome to share when you are finished. Ask them if that would be OK. The question offers them some option of choice or responsibility toward a sense of boundaries. It provides the possibility for them to be aware that there are two individuals who are participating. When you are finished sharing, then invite that person to speak and partake as a coequal. You might ask them some questions to encourage further interactions while you practice appropriate boundaries with your own role. Acknowledge what they have offered and thank them.

WHAT IS IMPATIENCE?

Impatience begins when a person primarily identifies with their own approach to a situation, perspectives, feelings, timeline, and then projects one or more of these onto another person, expecting that the other should participate with the same choices and understanding. This behavior blocks the possibility of discovery and authentic sharing with someone else. It is a domineering approach; there is no opportunity to discover the unique individuality of another. Once impatience is activated, judgement and resistance against the other person ensue. It creates a struggle and is an act of rejection toward the other person.

HOW CAN I CHALLENGE MY OWN IMPATIENCE?

First, bring your focus inward, and notice the details of what you are doing – be curious. Notice your beliefs. What other feelings do you have toward the other person or situation besides the impatience? Ask yourself, "Is it appropriate for me to want to push my beliefs, understanding, agenda, my way of doing things onto this other person or circumstance?"

You must allow for moments of stillness and space to exist within yourself. This happens naturally, when you function from a place of curiosity.

Now, while noticing who you are, create the intention to put yourself aside. Next, challenge yourself to witness who the other person really is, the details of the circumstances that are taking place, and put in the effort to share in the uniqueness of the experience. You can be present as an individual, without a struggle, when you recognize and negotiate through the real happenings and possibilities within any situation. The process of these steps naturally creates respectful, individual boundaries.

WHAT IS SHAME?

This is an emotional state that helps us to gauge or monitor the effects of our choices and actions with self and others. It helps us to create personal accountability. It lets us know when we need to reevaluate our intentions and understanding, so that we can redirect ourselves in purposeful choice with awareness of its relationship to outcome. Shame can create direction and movement for "process" and learning. This can be a powerful tool to help reset our thinking and understanding.

A healthy understanding and means of making sense of shame must be learned. Otherwise, the possibility or activation of it will create fear or the desire to flee, or there will be attempts to dominate or escape from it through self-righteousness or disassociation. If this does not temporarily fulfill the individual's needs, they may then attempt to transfer it onto someone else through judgement, blame, and anger. In this scenario, the person unconsciously imagines someone else to be wrong, with the possibility of shame existing in that person instead of themselves. Ultimately, when someone has not learned how to make sense of shame through purposeful "process," it will have no useful road to travel. One's dead-end experience will translate into the perception of being bad or broken, while leaving the person with no option for resolving it.

HOW CAN I OVERCOME UNHEALTHY SHAME?

Know that you have been lingering in conflict from the shame because you did not learn how to understand it or respond to it in a purposeful way. When it gets triggered, notice the feelings that you have when it rises within you. Are you afraid? Do you feel trapped in the idea of being wrong? Do you want to blame someone else? Is there a belief that you cannot stand on your own, in your own truth? Did you make a mistake and do you not know what to do next? Do you feel as though you are or could be rejected, shunned, or discarded? Know that these feelings come from a basis of your incomplete programming. When you feel afraid, there is a tendency to want to escape from the shame instead of participating with it. When you participate with this feeling, as well as all others, you will become wiser.

When you consider real-life experiences and all your possibilities, some of the feelings you are experiencing will be true for you, and some of the beliefs within the feelings are probably untrue. Untrue beliefs can lead to false feelings.

Shame is just part of a process that can direct you inward to realize what you already know and don't know. Through inward participation with shame, a doorway gets created, so that one can access wisdom through a different choice and learning. Inward inquiry with shame can assist one to recognize personal responsibility with choice and outcome.

When you take an honest look within, what do you see? If you know for sure that someone else is falsely deciding that you are wrong, acknowledge that the thoughts and perspectives that are created by someone else belong to them. Is someone else blaming you for something to avoid taking responsibility themselves or to gain attention? If this is the case, know that a lie is a lie and just because someone says something, it does not make it true. You need only put your focus on what is real within you and validate it – celebrate it! Someone else's thoughts cannot decide anything for you or alter your identity. You are the only one who can see yourself clearly through inner inquiry and decide whether you have made purposeful choices or whether the choices need to be improved upon.

On the other hand, you must also ask yourself, "Did I intend to cause harm to myself or someone else?" Have you made conscious or unconscious choices that have created struggle or unintended pain for someone else? If you see that intentional or unintentional harm has taken place because of your decisions, then you must accept it and take responsibility for the outcome. You must do this to free yourself from the shame, to learn, and to move on. Ask for forgiveness from others and forgive yourself. Allow the new understanding and knowledge to be received with gratitude. If you reject the truth, then your mind will just keep going around in a struggle. Once you accept responsibility, look at what you have learned from the experience, accept the wisdom, and integrate it into your ongoing choices.

A sense of safety with the unfolding choices of life will then develop. When you realize the truth of your own individuality, along with a process to make sense of a conscious practice for personal choice, cause and effect, and an ability to recognize that the behaviors and perspectives of others are their own responsibility and yours belong to you, then natural boundaries are created. A healthy relationship with shame encourages the possibility of being renewed and nurtured by life, receiving from life. Each one of us is accountable for our own lives. If you look deep within your own place of stillness, you will find answers amidst the self – the Divine self. Divine truth exists within the essence of "All."

WHAT IS BLAME?

Blame suggests the idea of conscious fault. This is fitting when someone consciously decides to create an injustice or cause harm to another person. This would be an outright malicious act. Healthy blame identifies a place for relevant responsibility. However, a lot of the time accusations are inappropriately applied and inaccurately perceived.

Blame is often wrongly suggested in situations that involve active personalizing, dramatization, competition, entitlement, co-dependency, narcissism, and shame. It happens quite often. This occurs most frequently when boundaries are confused or unknown regarding individuality and personal responsibility. In these situations, there can be a lot of imaginary ideas projected, which suggest that other people understand what they are doing, when they do not, and perhaps are not even capable of knowing. Along with those projections come ideas of should have's, could have's, or why not's.

There is a lot of confusion around individual responsibility. Inappropriate blame presumes that others should know something that they haven't yet learned, and that they should be participating more clearly for you than you are for yourself. How could that be? You are the only one inside of you who has a cumulative experience that is unique to you alone. You are the only one who has the possibility of perceiving clearly for yourself, choosing for yourself, and creating a life that works for you. If you are anchored in your own individuality, and can see the truth of the moment with a clear perception of boundaries, then more often than not, you will perceive clearly for yourself. It still won't be perfect – there is no such thing.

HOW CAN I CHALLENGE MYSELF TO STOP BLAMING AND TO STOP TAKING ON THE BLAME FROM OTHERS?

If you are blaming someone else for something, bring your focus inward. Notice the details of your thoughts within the blame. Notice what your thoughts might be suggesting. Notice the beliefs. Are you wanting someone else to see your needs and take care of you when you are not choosing to do what you need in order to take care of yourself? Are you expecting others to take on your life process for you? Are you expecting others to know things that you are not clearly communicating? If this is the case, then ask yourself if this is reasonable, fair, or respectful toward yourself or others. Continue with the questions. What am I doing that is not working? Am I willing to make different choices to figure it out? Do I want to be responsible for my own life, or do I want to continue pretending that someone else should be responsible for me? Now take action to challenge your beliefs, to participate more fully and discover what you don't know. Replace your projections with new choices and direct your own firsthand experiences.

If someone else is blaming you, once again, bring your focus inward. Notice your emotional responses to the blame. What are your beliefs? Are they true or untrue? Perhaps the other person is suggesting that you should have known their desires or is implying that you could have rescued them in a difficult situation. Maybe they are telling themselves stories and imagining you had a role that did not even exist. Maybe your belief is that you feel guilty because you did not sacrifice yourself to rescue them. Maybe you feel that they should know that their entitled suggestions are wrong. Challenge your own beliefs. Look at what might be missing from your interactions. Ask yourself where your responsibilities exist and don't exist. If you have made an inappropriate choice, then accept the reality and learn from it. Ask for forgiveness and forgive yourself. Be grateful that you have clarity and have learned something. Redirect your thoughts and choices appropriately.

To address this further, in a shared situation as described above, you could ask the other person questions about their suggestions. Then continue with more questions that direct them toward the larger picture of reality. Do this in an inquiring and curious way, not in a suggestive manner. The purpose of this process is to gather information that you may be unaware of and then to create boundaries based on what you see or don't see. It is not your goal to make the person see themselves or to change them. In the end, the other person may not gain any further clarity with themselves. The intent, rather, is for greater certainty of facts, so that you can make the best choices for yourself. Again, evaluate your perspective around responsibility toward self and the other person. Then redirect your role with it appropriately.

WHAT DOES IT MEAN TO FORGIVE?

The act of forgiving takes place when a person lets go of the attachment to judgement, ill will, or condemnation of someone who carried out a wrong. The person who was mistreated will no longer have an active blaming, defensive, retaliatory, or mental/emotional struggle in relation to the inappropriate behavior or action of the offender. This does not mean that the one who was wronged suddenly decides to excuse or diminish the seriousness of the transgression or continues to be subjected to harmful behavior. In fact, when the offense is habitual, then it would be wise to remove yourself from it.

If the offender does not acknowledge the injustice or express remorse, and continues to act in a harmful way, then a continued connection is probably not advisable. To carry on would be to both enable the wrongdoer and to disrespect yourself by allowing more harm to take place. If one falls prey to repeated acts of harm, then the act of forgiveness will be difficult or not likely. Healthy boundaries are essential.

If you played a part that allowed for ongoing harm to take place, then you must take responsibility for your part. Perhaps you unrealistically expected the other person's behavior to change despite their ongoing bad behavior. In this situation, you must also forgive yourself. Additionally, there will always be something for you to learn from every experience. If you look within, identify and internalize the lessons, then wisdom, forgiveness, and compassion will come to you more easily.

On the other hand, if the wrongdoer takes responsibility for a wrongdoing, and has regret, if learning takes place, and they no longer continue with the behavior, then there is a probability for a healthy ongoing connection. When someone makes an error in judgement, this is an opportunity for more learning. Making mistakes and not knowing are a part of life. At times "not knowing" has an inherent innocence in it. It is an opportunity to receive from the unknown, gain new understanding, and expand one's wisdom. When people consciously share in their mistakes and learn together, while having respect for individuality, then greater trust and intimacy are developed.

Sometimes there are reasons why it is difficult to forgive. Perhaps you live with the person in question and you really don't trust them. On some level, you feel that to forgive them would be to give up some sense of control that you think you have over the other individual. Maybe you worry that complete reconciliation would give them permission to repeat the harmful behavior. Under these circumstances, you will not be open to fully share. Anger, judgement, and resentment will act as a barrier or create a sense of guardedness that will not allow for a free flowing authentic exchange to take place. It is not possible to make choices for or manage another person. You just need to clearly communicate where you stand with your own feelings, needs, and boundaries. No matter what you think or want, the other individual will still be whoever they are inside. You will have to decide if the possible rewards of unhindered participation might outweigh the anticipated risk. If you allow a fear to govern you, then you will not have peace. When you allow yourself to participate in what is new, instead of being focused in the past, you can make choices according to what works for you as each new experience takes place. In this way, you are receiving the fullness of your experience while providing safety for yourself.

WHAT IS THE "EXPERIENTIAL SELF?"

The mind is the thinking, theorizing self. On the other hand, feelings, intuition, deep knowing, and Divine consciousness are the substance of the experiential self. If the mind were to exist without experience, there would be no sense of life – no true knowing. If something is created only with the mind, it cannot be anything more than an idea – a theory. Ideas alone are compartmentalized and empty of life. The experiential self is realized when one is fully present in the moment, free of projections and desires. We all have the capacity for this some of the time. In the moment experience brings clarity for purposeful choice and honest participation. This is the experience of wholeness and oneness with the Divine.

Conceptual understanding brings theory; whereas, experiential understanding brings knowing.

WHAT IS DIVINE CONSCIOUSNESS?

This is your pure essence – the substance of all. It is the truth and the light that is God, Great Spirit, Mother Earth, Jesus, Buddha, and/or Omnipresent Consciousness. It is the constant life force energy within you. It is the wind, the sky, the trees, the plants, and the animals. It is sustainable, limitless, and is all possibilities. This is your all-knowing guiding presence within. Wherever you put your focus, it determines what your experience will be. When it is focused in pure truth, it is in the Divine.

WHAT IS HEALTHY INDIVIDUAL IDENTITY?

When one is functioning in healthy individuality, there is honesty with oneself and others – a sharing in what is joyful and what is painful along with everything in between. A person will share in the similarities with another person while respecting the differences. There is an openness to discover and learn, along with personal respect and celebration of self. When something is not appropriate or is unhealthy, then the person does not participate. Healthy boundaries are made. One invites others to share with them while giving and receiving in authentic ways. A person takes responsibility for themselves and does not take responsibility for others in a sacrificial or enabling manner. When healthy programming is present, it is natural to challenge what doesn't work with an openness to discover and learn more.

Through participation in life, one's identity becomes multi-faceted. One recognizes and participates in multiple levels of experience: spiritual, intimate, social, practical, adventurous, fun-loving, creative, professional, etc. For balance to be in place, all levels must be fulfilled through some degree of participation.

HOW CAN I SUPPORT HEALTHY IDENTITY IN MYSELF?

Be honest with yourself and others. Ask for what you want. Let it be known when you don't want something. Do not pretend or hide yourself. Let others see your true self, so that you know whom you really connect with and who connects with you. There will always be people who don't like you – whether you are pretending or not. For someone who is transitioning out of addictive behaviors into health, it is very important to have a relationship with self and life on many levels. It is through participation that one builds relationships, confidence, and personal trust, and discovers likes and dislikes, develops skills and abilities, challenges the self, learns, and creates goals.

Take steps toward the fulfillment of your own intentions; recognize that every step is just part of the process.

Take responsibility by staying committed through the unpleasant and pleasant. An active Will, healthy Fierceness, and curiosity are your participatory tools and momentum for discovering and building individual identity.

WHERE IS THE TRUE FOUNDATION OF INDIVIDUAL TRUST?

This exists in large part within one's own personal relationship with the self. When you are honest with yourself and other people, the best available choices are likely to be utilized. If someone else is making a choice in relation to a shared situation and it does not work for you, then it is up to you to make a new choice for yourself or create a boundary. Never assume that someone else will understand who you are if you are not sharing your thoughts, needs, perspectives, likes, and dislikes. Even when you do share your preferences or needs, someone else will often choose in ways that will not make you happy. You are the only one who is inside of you. Others can only glimpse the fragments of experiences that you choose to share. Even then, someone else's interpretation of you will come from their own cumulative life history – their own way of defining information. Therefore, you must choose for yourself. In this way, you will be participating in self-love and personal respect.

Also, avoid falling into fantasies and false expectations around who you think someone else should be, when their behavior has shown you otherwise. You must pay attention to what is real instead of what you hope will happen. It is essential that you do not leave your choices in the hands of another person. If you do, your needs will be met by chance. If you avoid taking responsibility for yourself by avoiding the option of appropriate choice, then you will be disrespecting others, as well as yourself – your own possibilities, and your direct connection with life. This will only lead to a sense of powerlessness, struggle, blame, and a mix of difficult emotions. Each of us must be accountable for ourselves through choice, action, discovery, and creation in order to know and trust who we can be in our own lives.

Section Two

Tools for personal transformation

Tools for personal transformation

WHAT ARE THE WILL AND FIERCENESS?

THE SUBSTANCE OF WILL IS an inner strength, a staying power that becomes activated by concrete decision. Its driving force is a person's **Fierceness**. They go hand in hand and can be utilized for either supporting or harming the self and one's life experience. They are of the most benefit when directed in conscious, purposeful ways.

The **Will** can be recognized when one feels confidently or stubbornly strong in a perception or choice, which can be part of a theory or active experience. The Fierceness is the fire that creates motion to bring life or struggle to the Will. If healthy Fierceness is not in place, then the Will cannot be productive. For success to take place, the Will and Fierceness must be anchored in truth.

Fierceness can be recognized when an intensity of determination and motivation are present. Healthy Fierceness has courage in it. Courage is the part of Fierceness that allows it to step out into the unknown. When Fierceness gets stuck, it is often fueled by fear. When fear is behind Fierceness, it most often turns into stubbornness and anger. This can be very destructive as it cycles and intensifies.

One's Will and Fierceness are very important tools for personal discovery and growth. They can be applied in helpful or destructive ways. If Will and Fierceness are applied to one's intentions, ideas, or perceptions in a conscious purposeful manner with flexibility, then the creative process is stimulated. When steps are taken to fulfill one's purposeful intentions, then passion can be the end result.

Healthy fierceness builds and supports, while unhealthy fierceness breaks down and destroys.

WHAT DO DESTRUCTIVE WILL AND FIERCENESS LOOK LIKE?

The negative aspect of these abilities/tools can be recognized in behaviors such as stubbornness, rebellion, vengefulness, self-righteousness, and controlling or abusive anger. If they are applied in these forceful ways, then a person will feel stuck; damage can result, and the struggle will create a disconnect with the authentic self. These behaviors can also cause separation between individuals and/or situations. The effect is one of fleeting power where projected ideas replace honest discovery. This dynamic does not allow for a mutually shared experience of equality with healthy boundaries in place. If the Will and Fierceness are used to activate resistance toward discovery, new understanding, or learning, then the result will be a cycle of struggle that recurs over and over, a self-created trap.

WHERE DO I FIND MY WILL AND FIERCENESS?

Everyone has developed some degree of Will and Fierceness. The Will can be identified when one commits to a choice, idea, or understanding of something. It is the *act* of committing to the choice or experience. The Will is also integrated in the act of tolerating a choice and the act of taking ongoing steps. When you are doing something, you've chosen it either consciously or unconsciously; your Will is involved. Fierceness can be identified through focused, driven action or fixed resistance. You might recognize it in the energy of active passion, motivation, actions to protect, or in vengeful anger. It is the fire that carries you through an experience or keeps you stuck in something such as rebellion. At one end of the pole, behaviors such as stubbornness or resistance encompass a frozen quality of both Will and Fierceness. On the opposite end of the pole passion and determination encompass both Will and Fierceness in action. If you are not familiar with these tools, you will have to create the intention to consciously witness them within yourself and then consciously put them into motion through purposeful choice.

HOW DO I ACTIVATE MY WILL AND FIERCENESS?

Understanding what these capabilities are, and how they can benefit you, is your first step toward their use and activation. Now, recall a memory that has these abilities active in it. Feel the nature of the active Will and Fierceness as you focus on the memory. Notice how charged they feel. While they feel charged, transfer them into your present intention, idea, or plan. Identify a "first step" toward completion of your goal. It is important to take a step or some steps toward the fulfillment of your idea; otherwise, you may get stuck. Motion is created through participation. Always be open to perceive the next step, and be ready to take it if possible; otherwise, it may become a piece of a theory. An awareness of subsequent steps often comes through participation with the present moment's step. You just need one step at a time. Do not try to force the steps; otherwise, you could get caught up in a struggle. Sometimes there will be stillness between steps. This is when more undirected unfolding occurs and reflection can take place. This leaves room for wisdom, ideas, and creativity to surface. As you proceed, the momentum most often increases.

WHAT DOES IT MEAN TO WITNESS?

One must be able to see the self in order to discover, learn, and change. If a person habitually has resistance and fear toward change, or disguises the true self, then they are not clear about how to witness the self. One must also be able to see or witness possibilities without prejudging or avoiding them, so that considering a choice is possible.

Witnessing takes place when one just watches an occurrence or situation within the self or one's surroundings without trying to direct it. One chooses to be free from consciously engaging in desire, attachment, expectation, judgement, or a particular role or goal. However, the subconscious mind may still function from various levels of attachment. You will be watching it and gaining clarity instead of adding an additional layer of struggle to your inner or outer experience. It is like stepping back and simply noticing. It allows one to "see" and understand more of oneself or another. Witnessing allows for the authenticity of the experience to have a cleaner presentation. It is like watching a bird in a tree; and then, while having no attachment, just patiently waiting to see what happens next. The experience being witnessed is independent of any attachment or role that you may typically create.

It is common for the ability to witness to be activated unconsciously, when behaviors that challenge one's sense of right and wrong occur. An example of this that most people can identify with is from a situation when they tell a lie. They know that they are telling a lie, and they watch

themselves carry it out. A mix of emotions may play out
at the same time – a little fear, some strategizing, the desire to succeed, or regret for lying, and maybe some shame
and guilt. That "watching" part of the self is the conscious
spiritual "I AM" level that can recognize truth. Witnessing
is not only an effective tool, but a doorway to your Divine
self or spiritual consciousness.

How do I enter the witnessing process?

In order to transition from an attached or reactive mode
into a witnessing approach, one needs to consciously and
honestly acknowledge what is taking place in an experience or struggle. For example, one may inwardly state, "I
see myself getting angry and wanting to blame that other
person for what I am feeling. Am I responsible for what I
am feeling, or is that other person responsible for what I
am feeling? Can I choose my own feelings, or can another
sneak inside of me and force me to choose in a certain way?
Am I imagining that that person's choices can decide my
experience for me? In what purposeful way can I direct my
focus and create my own experience right now?"

This process of curiosity and inquiry begins to create
some space around the consuming effects of your reaction
or attachment. Keep going with this and become even more
curious. As you allow for open ended questions from within
the curious state, your consciousness can show you more of

the stored or activated components of your psyche: personal beliefs, roles, desires, old traumas, and new possibilities.

When this is done in a meditation practice, it is done without questions. One just notices the thoughts that come and go, without creating any interaction with the thoughts.

WHAT DOES IT MEAN TO SURRENDER?

To surrender is to put desire and expectation aside. This allows a person to be in an experience in an authentic receptive way, rather than being on the outside of it in a controlling manner. If one is attached to the idea of things playing out in a certain way, and things don't proceed in the anticipated manner, an inner struggle or turmoil can get created. Resistance or attachment will result. This blocks one's ability to be fully present with the possibilities that are available for the choosing. When a person is present in the natural unfolding of a situation, if an opportunity presents itself, one will see it. On the other hand, if an option for a desired outcome does not present itself, then one will be aware of this as well. It will be what it will be.

HOW DOES ONE SURRENDER?

In a state of surrender, one lets go of all attachment to anything specific occurring within an experience. There is no attempt to control or force a sequence of events or to make anything happen. Within surrender, or a state of just being, there is a natural unfolding. The ego is not in charge. One's basic experience, idea, or feeling exists freely in the open space of one's awareness. There is a stillness present. If you are having difficulty with this concept, then activate your feeling of curiosity with an intention to just watch your inner experience. It can be helpful to use curiosity as a tool. Just relax into it. This supports a transition into a cleaner state of surrender. Curiosity is naturally open- ended. It creates a doorway for the unknown to be received in nongrasping ways. Since it is nonspecific and nongrasping, it invites the experience to transform as visions or insights arise. The curiosity will eventually fall away. The natural movement of the experience just takes place without having anything direct it. If curiosity were to remain a part of it, this would be a creative process.

WHAT IS A STATE OF CREATIVE PROCESS?

This takes place when one has surrendered, is unattached – free of any sense of grasping. One has surrendered into the substance of an experience with an open-ended intention or question. Curiosity is active and present; an unattached openness exists within any inquiry. The experience leads the way without having the mind direct it. A state of curiosity, along with surrender, creates space for the unknown and allows insight and visions to immerge. Insight and visions may arise in steps or through a sense of experiential knowing.

WHAT ARE ANALYSIS, REFLECTION, AND CURIOSITY?

Analysis involves a process of the conscious mind digging into an experience to extract or dissect its parts and decide the relationship between the parts. This also involves determining the relationship between the experience being analyzed and a theory, label, or designated category.

Reflection takes place more in the experiential self than in the mind. When you recall something through reflection, you bring it back into your active inner experience through your ability to witness. However, there is no categorization or judgement or force applied. The experience is taken on, but is not personalized or contained. It does not consume or dominate the sense of self. This is a graceful, neutral state that allows a person to try things on in various ways and wisdom to come forth.

Curiosity is a state of being that creates an invitation or opening for the unknown to come forth and be discovered. There is no attachment to know something in a certain way. It is an innocent, welcoming, receptive mode that includes a patient stillness and the aptitude to witness. There is an element of surrender woven into it.

Section Three

Understanding the process
for transformation

Understanding the process for transformation

HOW DOES ONE BEGIN THE PROCESS OF TRANSFORMATION?

LOCATE A GOOD SOURCE OF support for your choice to move forward in truth. If you have an active substance addiction along with addictive behaviors, your first step will be to eliminate the chemical, perhaps through a detox program. Then, for all situations of addictive behavior, I would also recommend a therapist (conventional or holistic) and/or assistance from a wise individual whom you know and trust, a support group (twelve step programs can be very helpful), or a spiritual community. Your number one source of support comes from you. Through your commitment to personal honesty and discovery, you will come to know and trust yourself. Only through knowing yourself can you help yourself. Initially, honest participation with the self can be a scary experience. It may trigger shame, guilt, blame, anger, sadness, etc. All of these feelings are natural. You can make friends with them as you learn what healthy emotional boundaries are and come to know your authentic self. Know that, as you direct your focus inward, all of your feelings can become doorways for accessing your own innate wisdom and strength. Your awareness of self is uncovered a step at a time – just like everything else. This equals "process."

It is important to know that you never get rid of anything within the self; it gets transformed through acknowledgment of truth, activation of new choices, forward movement, and practice. You need only add to what is already within you and it will transform. Any understanding of the mind only becomes a true knowing as you practice participating with that understanding until it becomes your own. At this point, it is a true knowing.

One of the obstacles that you may encounter is resistance. The ego will try to hold onto what it knows, and what is familiar: fear, anger, sadness, impatience, etc. The ego will also try to keep you in black-and-white, either/or thinking, in order to sabotage your efforts. If you understand what is happening, then it becomes a little easier to challenge it and participate within a deeper level of experience. Know that it is much safer to witness and experience an emotional state than it is to act it out in a place where it does not belong.

In order to know and understand yourself, you need to know how to see or witness who you are on the inside. So often, when people are in need, they keep their focus primarily on their outer experience, which only makes apparent a piece of any reality. This will bring about a distorted perception and an inner struggle. As an example, if you dislike the outcome of a choice that is made by another person and stay outwardly focused, then you are likely to feel powerless and dependent on that person. However, if you acknowledge the disappointment, then notice your own reactions, beliefs, responsibilities, and new possibilities, you are likely to make new choices and discoveries. When one is in the process of making conscious choices to transition limiting behaviors and perceptions, it is important to bring the focus inward to view whatever discomforts or beliefs arise within your own consciousness. In this way, untrue beliefs and the layers of harmful or limiting patterns of behavior can be seen with greater clarity. The tools of curiosity, witnessing, Fierceness, and surrender are embraced through mindful participation with self. Individuals cannot fully process an experience until they see what is within themselves and what is equally in their outer experiences along with new possibilities. You must allow yourself to see the actual details of an inner or outer experience without distorting it with imagined desirable or undesirable details. When you realize where your own experience, responsibilities, abilities, and incapability's begin and end, it becomes easier to have consistent movement with goals or intentions. A state of stillness and the spontaneous unfolding of experience will also become more comfortable and make more sense. One's personal/ emotional boundaries can also be actualized.

WHAT MIGHT A PROCESS FOR CHANGE LOOK LIKE?

At first, through self-observation, you gain some understanding of what is happening with your inner self. With the use of reflection and curiosity, you will be able to identify a behavior that no longer works for you, along with some alternate possibilities and choices. You decide upon a first step. Then you proceed with your choice. This will activate the process of discovery. You make discoveries, integrate the wisdom, and then make more choices. You will not know all of the steps at once; nor will your situation change all at once. After you take each step, reflect and notice what is or is not useful, what else is needed, etc. Each time you take a new step, you will learn something about yourself and the possibilities within your goal. The outcome of each choice never takes place exactly as you envision it. This is where surrender and flexibility are necessary.

Sometimes, when the behavior that needs changing gets triggered, you may or may not remember to challenge it with your new intention. It's all OK. When you are able to apply yourself in a new step or repeated steps, be sure to consciously acknowledge your success. In this way, you are offering your subconscious mind a reward. When you don't remember to choose differently in the moment, but realize this after the fact, a little disappointment can help you to further activate your tools of Will and Fierceness. This can help you to reinforce your commitment for change. The unfolding details of a natural process and an exact way of participation are not predictable. If you want to predict the exact outcome of each step, you will become resistant to taking steps. Be careful not to encourage black and white thinking through self-judgement. Instead, *celebrate your intention and each small accomplishment.* This is your way of loving and supporting yourself. The more you consciously celebrate each small success, the more likely you are to see more options in the moment. Through practice, you will get better and better until the new way becomes automatic most of the time. Know that your commitment to the process is where your strength lies. Just maintain your intention to stay open to new learning and keep going whenever you have a new awareness or recognize a new choice. No two learning experiences are alike; so be patient. Remember that whatever is happening today will be different tomorrow.

HOW DOES REPETITIOUS PARTICIPATION EFFECT LEARNING?

If something can be comprehended, it does not mean that it has been learned. Until an awareness or comprehension of facts has been *integrated* through repeated action into one's natural thinking processes, choices, and experience, it is only theory. When learning how to think, understand, and function in new ways, a commitment is needed, in the same way that a commitment is needed when learning to speak a foreign language, play a violin, ski, dance, etc. When one embarks upon the journey of change, consistent effort is needed until the goal is reached. This means practicing over and over again. It's best to have flexibility within each step while having no expectation of a timeline. Some of what you expect and do not expect will occur. As you learn, there will be moments of satisfaction, challenge, disappointment, discouragement, hope, fulfillment, and adventure. It all changes every day. Once a theory has been integrated through participation or practice, it becomes part of your foundation. However, there will always be an ever-changing quality within everything that you think you already know. This is why ongoing curiosity, reflection, and participation need to be a part of your everyday functioning. There is always room for every realization or accomplishment to keep growing. One must be careful not to interject black-and-white, either/or thinking into this process. If you do, your trust in self and the possibility for change can be interrupted or permanently sabotaged. Your learning and progress cannot take place in a concrete, predictable way. Be patient and kind to yourself.

Section Four

Mindful witnessing and healing practices

Mindful witnessing and healing practices

BASIC MINDFUL WITNESSING TECHNIQUE – OPTION ONE – SITTING OR LYING DOWN

TWO DIFFERENT OPTIONS ARE OFFERED for a basic technique. Either one can be used. The first one is appropriate for those who can be still and somewhat present with their experiential self. The second one may be more fitting for individuals who have very active minds and have difficulty being still. Both of these can be used for everyday practice. When you start, stay with it for five to ten minutes or as long as you can. Increase your practice time every couple of days. Your goal should be twenty to thirty minutes a day. Do the best that you can. Whatever you do is a success.

The goal is not to empty the mind, but instead to acknowledge any emotion or thought that arises. Just see it as it is and give it the freedom to just be. When you acknowledge the presence and movement of the various expressions of self, this will help you to be more aware of how to go inward to access the authentic self. This will bring some familiarity to the beginning stages of mindful processing in your everyday life.

Option one is as follows: This technique provides an opportunity for you to practice the skills of curiosity and witnessing, and to identify without personalizing. This will also teach you how to be familiar and comfortable with your inner space.

1. Find a quiet, warm, and comfortable place to sit or lie down. Position yourself with your head, neck, and back straight, yet relaxed.

2. Bring your focus inward while letting go of any need to do anything other than to notice. Curiosity can assist one in noticing and staying focused. This quality of experience has a state of surrender woven into it – it is open ended. Know that your focus will not be fixed on any thought or feeling in a rigid manner. The focus is relaxed, but steady. This takes practice.

3. Watch every thought, image, feeling, or fragmented scenario come and go. They will arise and they will do whatever they are going to do on their own. You just let go of any tendency or compulsion to have a role in controlling them. This is surrender. When thoughts or feelings present themselves, don't ignore or suppress them, just simply acknowledge them without adding anything to them or taking

anything away from them. Use your curiosity in a steady, yet flexible manner.

4. If you find yourself getting carried away by your thoughts, observe where your mind goes, without judging, and simply return to your watchful, curious state. Remember this is a process. Refrain from judging. Be easy on yourself – be patient.

5. As the time comes to a close, take a deep breath, open your eyes, and let yourself get acclimated to your surroundings.

BASIC MINDFUL WITNESSING TECHNIQUE – OPTION TWO – A WALKING PRACTICE

This mindful witnessing technique is intended to direct your focus to the spontaneous sensory experiences that occur while walking in slow rhythmic movements. This teaches one how to experience sensations and visuals in a clean, present-moment manner. This process can be done outside, preferably in a location that is free of road traffic, or it can even be done indoors. If you can choose an outdoor location, there is likely to be a greater variety of sensory stimuli. If this is not possible, one can apply this technique indoors while walking in circles. You will be noticing sensations and experiences from your body movements as well as from your sight, hearing, smell, and touch.

1. As you begin walking, slowly and rhythmically, notice the various sensations of movement in your legs, arms, and feet as they touch and lift from the ground. A greater earth connection is created if you wear soft soled shoes or go barefoot. Notice your breath as well, as it enters and leaves your body.

2. Now begin to notice other sensations that come through your senses. Be aware of the sound of a bird calling out, the sound of trees rustling in the breeze, the smell of dry earth, and the sound of dry leaves crunching underfoot. You might notice the color of the dirt, the texture of tree roots. Perhaps you see other people, hear them talking, feel your hair move against your skin, or the air moving in and out of your nostrils. You might smell the freshness of the air. Keep going.

3. Your mind simply acknowledges each experience while shifting focus from one level of your senses to the next. There is nothing being added or taken away from each occurrence – no memories, no associations, desires, or judgements. It is kept clean. The mind is kept busy in an unattached way, as it shifts the focus from one sensation to the next, then the next, and the next. There is a state of surrender and grace that is woven into this process. The ever-changing repetition of this experience creates a trance state. Your vibration will become one with your surroundings. The ego is not active. You are in the moment.

4. Practice this often. In the beginning, you will be directing your experience through conscious intention and effort. It will take effort because it is not yet familiar. Soon it will become an automatic, natural process; you will feel the surrender, grace, and bliss that comes from being in the moment. If you become synchronized with the forest, the animals will perceive you as an equal. They will be unaffected by your presence. Even though you are there, they will go about their business in a relaxed way.

Practice one or both of these basic approaches repeatedly, until you feel confident and then, if you choose, you can go on to the next technique.

A MINDFUL PROCESS FOR TRANSITIONING OUT OF COMPULSIONS

Once you are familiar with the practice of mindfully witnessing and acknowledging your everyday inner thoughts and feelings, you will have created some awareness of inner space. It will now be easier to access the substance of your compulsions. To do this, begin with the same approach that you use for the mindful witnessing technique for everyday use.

1. Bring your focus inward while experiencing and noticing the compulsion. Refrain from dissecting

it – just be with it. There will be feelings within it. Notice them as they are shown to you through the witnessing. Let yourself fully experience each one of the feelings. See and feel whatever is there, but do not add anything to it or take anything away from it. *You are giving it space to reveal itself and do what it will do.* This will have to be repeated many times.

2. Some examples of what you might be feeling are as follows: "I feel an urgency to take quick action; I am anticipating excitement from the idea of fulfilling the action; I am feeling anxiety and the need to get rid of it through the compulsive action; I am feeling self-conscious and inadequate." The witnessing and acknowledging can put some space between you and the power of the compulsion. It will bring you to a deeper part of your inner conflict and begin to reduce the desire within it. As you invite each feeling you are giving it the freedom to process, to do what it needs to do, to play out, while wisdom and understanding are unearthed from within.

3. Next, ask some questions that will challenge the compulsion and expand the experience outward into a larger reality. Through your participation with questions, the compulsion can become expanded and connect to an awareness of cause and effect, action and consequence, and need and possibilities. You don't get rid of it. You add more to it. It expands into

the larger reality and it naturally transforms step by step. This process takes time and repeated effort.

4. Some examples of questions to ask of your inner self could be as follows: "Why do I have this urgency? Is it in my best interest to follow through with the it? What might the outcome be? If I choose to act on this, how will I feel after the fact? Are there other ways that I can deal with the anxiety and the feeling of wanting to escape? What other options might I explore? Is there an alternate step that I can take right now?" Stay with this process until the charge in the compulsion feels diminished to some degree. After each question, be still inside so that you create some space for your consciousness to respond. Do not try to force a response – just let it come to you.

5. During this process you will encounter resistance from within. When this happens, bring your focus and curiosity inward to invite and witness the full experience of the resistance. You will notice that it is made up of judgement and some kind of insecurity or self-righteousness about what has been, what could be, or what might not be. Know that you are creating all of this subconsciously. You are the one who can decide to walk through the resistance and to keep going with purposeful choices.

6. If you are finding it difficult to identify with the compulsion from a place of strength, or you feel

powerless as you witness, then bring your focus to the aspect of self that is witnessing or watching. Ask yourself, "Who is the one who is witnessing? Who is that? I feel the compulsion, but I am also aware of the consciousness within me that is witnessing." Keep doing this and the presence of the witnessing consciousness within will become greater. The watching level of consciousness within is your Divine Essence or All-knowing Consciousness. Notice how this aspect of you "just is." There is no struggle there. This level of self is constant, dependable, and clean. This is where you find your authentic support within.

Every time a compulsion is challenged, this act will take a little more power away from it, contributing to a cumulative effect. As this happens, your overall experience of the compulsion becomes more conscious. This means that you will have more space or room in your mind to make choices in relation to the impulses. The more you connect the compulsion to rational inquiry, cause and effect, and new options, the more anchored it becomes there, until it finally transitions from a dominating force into a simple desire that is accompanied by the possibilities of choice.

7. Once you have developed some confidence in your ability to create space around a compulsion, you can create the intention to redirect your focus and

participation into something purposeful. At this point, you will begin to do this some of the time in your day to day life. Since it can sometimes be difficult to identify an on-the-spot alternate option, it is a good idea to make a list of purposeful choices. Keep the list handy so that you can refer to it when the need arises. Purposeful choices are actions that have a meaningful or beneficial effect on your life. It could be something as small as changing a light bulb, sewing on a button, sending an email, or making a cup of tea. Or it may be something more, like taking a walk, praying, cooking a nice meal, calling or visiting a friend, planning a trip, researching something of interest, looking for a new job, or doing a project or some artwork. All of these things can add something of quality to your life experience, whereas a compulsive act will not. Compulsions separate you from the wholeness of experience and a multitude of possibilities.

Your commitment to a consistent practice of witnessing is needed for results. Don't expect the thought or idea to instantly transition into a new reality. That concept is the language of the compulsive, black and white programming. True knowing comes from taking many steps which transition one experience into another as innate understanding and awareness arise.

A MINDFUL APPROACH TO HELP YOU TO TRANSITION OUT OF A WORRIED STATE

This inner process can assist you in transitioning from one level of concern or worry into a more functional, grounded level of inner experience. This will also help you to determine clearer boundaries and options with yourself and your situation.

To begin this process, it is necessary to put your focus on your inner experience without having a role connected to it. You just watch what is happening. Use your curiosity to witness the inner happenings. If you are having trouble with that, engage your Fierceness as well. The Fierceness can initially be used as a tool for anchoring in your determination to start the process. Once you are in a state of witnessing, as you begin to merge and move with your inner experience, the Fierceness can dissolve or fade away. At this point, you will have no agenda, make no judgements, apply no efforts to do anything about what you see. You may feel a sense of surrender and graceful movement. The following is an example of what might be happening with your thoughts as you acknowledge your inner experience.

"I see myself getting consumed by thoughts of worry. I am afraid. I am imagining the worst and playing out terrible scenarios, so that I can't think straight." Know that you can't do anything with the drama – it's fantasy. Drama will not create solutions. It only goes around and around.

If you choose to keep playing it out, you will just be further terrorizing yourself. As you witness, you create some internal space. This is the beginning of creating an internal boundary between the consuming effects of the reactive scenario or drama and your authentic self.

Continue to stay with the process. Let the experience lead you to a deeper level of truth – just observe. Then ask yourself a question, such as, "What has actually happened to trigger this worry?" Just experience what comes – do not analyze. An example of what you might see could look like this: "Initially my boss criticized me and made it clear that I have to do things his way." Then maybe you added many scenarios to it from your imagination such as, "I don't think that he likes me. Maybe they have plans to get rid of me. How will I pay my bills? Where will I get a job, etc.? I just now realize that I am creating judgement toward him."

So, you see that there was a basic truth, but with a lot of drama added to it. When you make a distinction between truth and drama, a natural boundary is created. Also, notice how the drama escalated into judgement. As judgement is removed, the substance and value of each experience can be realized. As you proceed, you might ask yourself, "Do I need to take any action or make a choice in relation to this basic truth?"

If you see real possibilities available, then make those choices. Otherwise, just let go and allow your situation to further unfold. Know that real choices do not exist in "what ifs" or "maybes." These are just extensions of imagination that have been added on to the basic situation. You might also ask, "What can I learn from this, and how can I apply that learning to my ongoing experience?" Now that you are refocused in the basic truth, you can make a further transition into a more stable experience of self.

At this point, direct your focus into your experience of individuality, acknowledging many of the different aspects of the self – creative, practical, spiritual, professional, intimate, adventurous, social, etc. As you acknowledge yourself through your values, abilities, challenges, qualities, likes, dislikes, and visions – *feel them. Feel the experience* of them, and at the same time, celebrate each piece of experience within. Let yourself feel gratitude. This approach is your tool for anchoring yourself into a safe, strong place. Revisit each part of authentic individuality numerous times. Once you feel anchored and more confident, bring your focus outward into your present moment experience and proceed with your day.

Note: You can use the same technique to witness your ongoing everyday experiences in the outer world. This approach will give you the space to more clearly see *what is actually happening and not happening.* You will see that it is possible to mindfully choose between reactive roles and purposeful sharing.

A MINDFUL WITNESSING APPROACH TO PROCESS TRIGGERED EMOTIONS

This approach is similar to the previous examples. First, you bring your focus inward to witness whatever is challenging you. Just let your attention be free flowing, without trying to contain anything. When you bring your focus inward, the attention within the focus directs a free-flowing energy to the fragmented experience. This unattached, fresh energy brings movement, which aids in a natural processing and transitioning. When you are present with the spontaneous inner expressions that arise, the experience itself will show you what you need to see – wisdom will surface. An understanding of each part of the experience arises, which transitions the fragmented parts into a state of wholeness and gratitude – a present state of being that is a place full of possibilities.

To begin this process, focus on the inner experience that is challenging you. Remember, you have no role here except to watch what is happening. Use your curiosity to witness the inner occurrences. If you are having trouble doing this, notice if there might be another less obvious layer of emotion: fear of fear, anger about fear, anger about anger, fear of sadness, resistance toward directly viewing a compulsion, stubbornness toward perceiving things in an honest way, etc. Know that being afraid of your fear feeds it. The same is true with any other multi-layered reaction – they feed on each other. If this is the case, first focus on the reaction to your reaction – such as the fear of fear – and then stay with it. Let it do whatever it is going to do and follow along. As you witness, there will be a sense of surrender, of merging, and of graceful movement within the experience.

Once again, you will have no agenda, no judgements, and make no effort to do anything with what you see. For example, someone gets angry at you, but you don't respond to it in the moment because you are afraid. Your second re-action comes later; you get angry at yourself for not speaking up. You start there with your attention – just watching. Let the emotion do whatever it is going to do, while simply witnessing and *feeling* it. A realization may be like this: "I am angry at myself because I'm afraid to speak up. I feel myself wanting to speak up. I'm realizing that I don't know how to speak up. I feel like no one will hear me if I speak up, so I want to blame the other person. I can see that I have my own feelings and viewpoints. Now, I understand that it's unfair to myself and the other person when I don't voice them. My experience is real. I can own it. I under-stand what is happening. I feel better now. I am grateful to see that I have my own option of choice."

Each level of experience emerges on its own as you watch and feel – there is no analyzing. You are not add-ing anything to the experience or taking anything away from it. Let yourself settle into the variations of emotion just like you would settle into a comfortable chair. There is no resistance. There is an invitation. If you give it your attention, then what is needed emerges from the experience. As you acknowledge each expression just as it is, you may feel lighter, and the original charge from the emotion can diminish or disappear. When you are working with multiple layers, one reaction will clear, then you may or may not find yourself in another active layer. Sometimes memories that seemed benign will connect to the feelings. There is often no conscious association between the memory and the feeling, but as this process takes place, a deeper understanding of self develops and wisdom integrates.

It often stands that many different memories have the same feeling on a foundational level. The essence is the same; the circumstances change. When experiences or traumas are unresolved, people will repetitiously create new scenarios to engage the original struggle. This leads to the development of behavior patterns and emotional defenses. As new situations compile, one upon another, the original experience often gets lost in the mix. The original feeling that is deep rooted in the compilation of situations must be accessed for the whole string to clear. As you go through this process of witnessing and receiving from your inner self, a natural dismantling, resolution, and integration can take place. Continuing onward, another layer could surface.

The following example shows how additional levels of challenges and realizations may unfold when you are witnessing and interacting with your inner experience. "This is the same feeling that I had when my father criticized me. It is as though he is condemning me right now and I feel powerless. I feel shame, feel broken, as though there is no way to make it right. But I now realize that there was no way to anticipate his next expectation, because I was not him. I realize that I now exist as an individual. I am real and I have my own separate experience. I am the only one who can see clearly for me. I feel relief in realizing that I can decide what is right for me now. The struggle is gone. I am grateful. I can make decisions for myself in my own life, without feeling that someone else's suggestions have already taken away my reality and decided things for me. I feel free of that now – I feel peace." To gain the full wisdom from an emotional pattern, the whole history or string of reactions must be cleared.

At this point, bring your focus back to the original situation. Put your attention on it to see if you feel any remaining charge from the original reactive emotions. The idea of it will still remain. This is okay. It's a memory. However, notice whether the emotional charge is gone. If so, then your mindful watching gave the reactive charge the space to process – to do whatever it needed to do – in order for the wisdom of your authentic self to rise up into your consciousness. If a charge is still present, it will probably be a lot less than it was initially. You can choose to go through the experience again or let it go for the time being. You might wait until a variation of it is triggered. The stronger the trigger, the more likely you will access the original programming. Why is this important? Understanding takes place through the mind. Change takes place through participation on an active experiential level. Your focus must be directed within the essence of your own active experience for transformation to occur.

CONCLUSION

Now THAT YOU HAVE A greater understanding of the "missing link" as it relates to your own behavior patterns, as well as an awareness of approaches and possibilities for change, you can move forward with your discovery of self. Remember that it is a process. Validate yourself at each step. Invite others in for support – to witness you, and to share in your truth. Practice the tools and use them. Be patient with yourself. This is a progression that requires repeated effort. It is up to you to apply yourself to the possibilities and invite the experience that comes from the steps of "seeking to discover." We are all meant to have the freedom of curiosity within us, so that we can receive from the unknown. We are all receivers for learning – for ongoing experience. It was never realistically meant to be that you instantly know things in life without participating as an individual. The idea of "just knowing" is part of the trap that comes from black and white thinking. As you participate with honesty in the present, a momentary knowing comes about, and then merges with your experiential history. As you take steps and create movement, segments of ongoing experience will transition with your experiential history and bring about a deeper understanding of yourself and your life.

You never have to get rid of anything; instead, you add more experience, understanding, and wisdom to what is already there. Then change occurs. What was there within you transitions into something new. This process consistently unfolds throughout your life. No one ever reaches a point in time when the discovery or learning is finished. A fixed state does not exist. Within you there is an experience of "All" which cannot be contained. There is freedom in the recognition of unlimited possibilities. That awareness will always bring more life – more substance and meaning within – never less. Life is a gift and you are an initiator in your own life. You need only take one step at a time. With each step, you build belief and trust in your own personal capabilities. Be confidently fierce – go out and discover! Create for yourself!

The nature of life and all its possibilities provides a dance between conscious, focused choice and spontaneous experience.